LAND OF
A MILLION MAGICIANS

An Abibigoro

Mohammed ben Abdallah

WOELI PUBLISHING SERVICES
ACCRA
1993

Published by
Woeli Publishing Services,
P.O. Box K601,
Accra New Town, Ghana

ISBN 9964-978-08-1

Editing, Typography and Design
W.A. Dekutsey
Typesetting
Mildred Vanderpuije
Cover Design
Amarquaye Adom

Printed by
Assemblies of God Literature Centre Ltd., Accra, Ghana.

For
Akosua Druye Amponsaa
Akosua Achaa Sa'adia
Aminata Akua Birago ... and the
the women and children of Nima
and Zongo!

This play was first produced in Accra, Ghana on 29th August, 1991 by Abibigoroma, a resident company of the Ghana National Theatre in collaboration with Abibiman Concert Party and Amore Cultural Troupe. The play was directed by Mohammed ben Abdallah who was assisted by William Addo. The music was provided by Lord Bob Cole while Atta Xornam Owusu choreographed the dances.

Characters

MUMMUNI, *A water seller*
OKOMFO
IMAM } *Gods in disguise*
CARDINAL
HASANA/FUSENI, *A prostitute later disguised as her twin brother*
CUSTOMER
FIRST I.R.S. MAN } *Tax Collectors*
SECOND I.R.S. MAN
MASTER OF CEREMONIES
MAGAJIYA, *Queen of the prostitutes*
FIRST TOKYO JOE
SECOND TOKYO JOE } *Ruffians*
THIRD TOKYO JOE
GROUNDNUT SELLER
FARM MANAGER
SUPERVISOR
PROPRIETOR
BUS DRIVER
ALHAJI, *A rich man*
HOUSING MANAGER
THREE WOMEN FROM NIIMAN
MUSICIANS, DANCERS, VENDORS, BEGGARS, etc.

A STREET IN NIIMAN

It is sunset on a Sunday. The busy street is awash with the soothing orange light of the setting sun. At various spots and on various levels are vendors of all sorts of food -- such as kenkey, kelewele, fried yam, and chinchinga. Various drinking and entertainment points are indicated by signs (neon and otherwise) — HARLEM CAFE, AGBAA LIQUOR BASE, DON'T MIND YOUR WIFE CHOP BAR; pharmacies, forex bureaux, etc., etc. There are various sounds and smells of the close of day. Deep in the background is a mixture — near confusion — of various sounds of the music and dance of the different indigenous groups that inhabit Niiman. Downstage, in a corner very close to the audience, a guitar band is playing for the enjoyment of passers-by who stop, listen, applaud, dance and occasionally drop some money into a collection hat. A sign in front of the guitar band reads ABIBIMAN CONCERT PARTY. In another corner, a Mallam (Muslim teacher) carrying a long whip supervises a group of young children as they repeat verses from the Qur'an *in an attempt to memorise them. Occasionally he uses the whip generously. MUMMUNI enters upstage. He is a middle-aged man who looks older than he really is. MUMMUNI carries across his shoulders a pole about three feet long with two water pots dangling from each of its ends. He notices the audience and bows to them..*

MUMMUNI

My name is Mummuni and this is Niiman, the city-within-a-city! I live here and I work here. What kind of work do I do? What kind question be that? You no get eyes? You no see what I de carry? I am Mummuni and I sell water. The people here in Niiman, they call me "Mai Ruwa." That's Hausa and

1

it means "Water-Man." No, no, no; it does not mean all the water in Niiman belongs to me, no! It only means I, Mummuni, son of Munkaila, I am nothing but a poor, common Water Seller! No, I am not complaining. How can I complain? Am I not the most popular "Mai Ruwa" in Niiman? When I pass here— it's "Mummuni." I pass there—it's "Mummuni! "Mai Ruwaa!"

The old women: "Mummuni!"

The young ones: "Mummuni!"

Even the very young who can barely walk or talk know how to connect this ugly face with Mummuni. So, I am not complaining ... Besides, who says I am the poorest man in Niiman? I am poor, yes! But that is the fashion here. We are all poor. Niiman is the land of the poor of the world. Maybe it is just an accident ... or vice versa, so to speak. As for today my English is flowing smoothly ... like Mma Shetu's okro soup! I believe I could have been a poet ... Anyway this is Niiman and you are all welcome. On behalf of the poor of the world, I, Mummuni, welcome you. If you are looking for the poorest Asante man, Ayigbe man, Dagomba man or even Kwawu man, they all live here. The "Ga Mantse" of the poor?... He lives just a few meters from here... Yoruba poor, Hausa poor, Soweto poor, Zimbabwe poor, the White man's poor — I mean Germans, Americans, and even English ...Them all dey here !!! They don't call this place "city-within-a-city" for nothing! Aaah, but today be Sunday and in Niiman Sunday means good time. You hear music everywhere! Abibiman Concert Party ... that's my favourite band, ... they are the ones playing over there by the cinema house. I like them. But I think today the hottest group in town are the Anago people ... the Yorubas. They have brought the famous Sonny Ade all the way from Lagos because Alhaji Bashiru Ayinde is naming his new-born child... And that group of

2

Anago people are dancing their way to the party ...

(A group of Yoruba men and women dance across the stage on their way to the naming ceremony.)

Today being Sunday, Niiman is full of music and dance. We may be poor in cash but I must say when it comes to the riches of the spirit, we are billionaires. We are full of the energy which is the source of life itself. Just take a look at our Ayigbe brothers and sisters. The Dahomeans of Benin.

(A spotlight picks up the Benin group in the middle of a vigorous dance.)

MUMMUNI

They make me wish I was young again. But oh, my brothers and sisters, if you have not seen Abu Kalangu, you haven't seen anything! Abu Kalangu is the master drummer of the Zongo people of Niiman.

(The spotlight picks up Zongo a group — led by ABU KALANGU and his small talking drum.)

That man performs wonders with that little drum. Do you see how he makes the drum talk to the dancers? How he makes them separate mind from body, limb from limb and set the body free! Look at that! Just look at those women ... Oh! God! I can't help myself ... please excuse me while I shake a bit ...

(He joins the group and dances with one of the women for a few minutes and then steps out of the group. The ZONGO GROUP fades out and, almost immediately, the ABIBIMAN CONCERT PARTY begins a new tune.

3

MUMMUNI recognises his favourite song immediately.)

MUMMUNI

Oh, ooh, my people! That's my song. That's my own favourite song: "Kukan Maraya" ... "The Song of the Orphan's Cry"... I must join them; I must sing with them...ooh!

(He joins the band and leads in singing that number. There is great excitement and dancing at the end of which MUMMUNI resumes the monologue ...)

You see, when I told you that our poverty has not destroyed our spirit ... I was not lying. When I say I am not complaining— in spite of my poverty — that too na true true. No be lie lie! But if I stand here and say I am not worried, my brother, that one na big lie! I am worried paa! Why? The gods! I am sure you are aware that we are supposed to be visited by gods! You see, reports reaching the Almighty about this land of ours is so bad that He, in His infinite wisdom, has decided to send three of His minor gods to come down here and conduct an on-the-spot inspection and investigation into our affairs. It has reached the long ears of the Almighty that we in this land ... you and I ... we are very bad! His numerous ears have told him that we are full of evil. He is aware that corruption, cheating, stealing, lying, fornication, murder, hypocrisy ... you name it... it is the order of the day in this precious land of ours. The Almighty is aware that in the dictionary of evil, there are seven deadly sins ... but that in this great land of ours, we have invented seventy-seven deadlier sins. There was a long debate in paradise to decide what should be done to us ... what unthinkable punishment to bring unto our heads and on the heads of our children and grand children even unto generations unborn. Many terrible punishments were suggested.

But the Almighty, in His infinite wisdom decided to give us a chance. He decided to send three of his most efficient and vigilant gods to come and espy the situation for themselves and give him an eye witness report. Now, why do you think I am worried? Look around! Just look around you! First of all, we all know they are coming. We don't know when, where or how. But we know they are coming! But have we mended our ways? Nooo! On the contrary, Crime, Evil, Corruption ... Badness in general is growing and multiplying at an unprecedented rate! As if that was not bad enough ... as if to add insult to injury NOBODY is making any preparations to receive the honourable gods! We are just busy being BAD! The authorities? You would expect at least the authorities to do something on behalf of the people. Oh, no! They are too busy to mind the gods. In fact, you know recently they have been renovating everything — roads, buildings, parks and gardens, conference rooms ... everything they see ... wham! ... they rehabilitate! ... No ... no ... no ... I have no objection to rehabilitation and construction ... after all they constructed this Niiman Highway ... now famous ... of course, they constructed it for themselves ... not for us... but to accelerate their speedy passage through this ... this ... this place to avoid the ugly sight and stench of poverty and squalor ... no ... seriously, it is very good. But why are they working so hard all over the place? Is it because the gods are coming? No!!! It is because of a special gathering of third world peoples! ... And, my brothers and sisters ... if you are looking for rehabilitation and road works, don't look here! After all Niiman is not where the delegates will visit! But knowing the way the Almighty works ... His ways being so strange... I bet the gods will choose to make their first appearance right here at Niiman!... Where we least expect them! .... When we least expect them! ... Perhaps disguised as some street-side dog chain sellers, or some wretched refugees! ... Oh my God ...

(He freezes.)

Oh! God what is this ...?

(He peers into the distance at three approaching figures.)

Oh! God, I see three strange characters approaching. Look! Just look at them! Shhh! Quiet. I don't want them to hear me! They look strange but they are not fooling me! A Traditional Priest in full regalia; a Cardinal in full costume; an Imam fresh from Mecca ... walking together? ... hand in hand? Impossible! It is them! My God, it is them! Help! Help! Shhh, quiet; Mummuni, calm down! Hold yourself together!

(The gods enter through the audience. They are costumed as described by MUMMUNI, each with his luggage. The "CARDINAL" carries an expensive looking suitcase, the "IMAM" has his luggage tied in a woollen blanket with a stick pushed through the knot of the blanket and he holds the stick in such a way that the bundle rests on his back. The OKOMFO has his belongings in a covered brass container which he carries on his head. They are obviously tired.)

OKOMFO

I thought you people said we were expected. I cannot go any further. I am tired and my feet are hurting.

IMAM

Oh, shut up! Stop complaining and come along. Anyway

6

whose fault is it that your feet hurt? Is it our fault that you insist on not wearing shoes?

OKOMFO
Whose idea was it that we should disguise ourselves in these ridiculous clothes? Wasn't it your idea?

CARDINAL
Oh, stop complaining! We are almost there. I can hear some music and plenty of noise ...

IMAM
Look over there! There is a man looking directly at us. He seems to be expecting us!

OKOMFO
My God! You are right; there are sounds of merriment and plenty of music. It seems there is one big party going on around here. I thought we were supposed to pick the poorest neighbourhood.

CARDINAL
This is the poorest neighbourhood, you fool! They are so poor they have to do something to keep their spirits up *(to MUMMUNI)* . Greetings, my son.

MUMMUNI
Greetings to you Respected Ones! You are most welcome.

IMAM
Salaam Alaikum!

MUMMUNI
Alaikum Salaam!

OKOMFO

Tell me my son, what place is this?

MUMMUNI

This is Niiman, Honourable Elders, the city-within-a-city. I
am Mummuni the water seller; and you are most welcome.

CARDINAL

Thank you my son. I see you have been expecting us. Are we
expected?

MUMMUNI

Err... yes...and er ... no... I mean yes! Honourable elders, what
I mean is: Er...who are you? I mean are you the gods we are
expecting?...

CARDINAL

Er...hem...er.

MUMMUNI

Of course, you are! Of course! What is the matter with me?
Please forgive me. Of course, you are the gods! And of course
I am ... I mean ... we are ... I mean you are expected.

IMAM

You see. I told you they have made preparations to receive us.
All those construction works, renovations and road repairs
going on ...

CARDINAL

My friends, don't deceive yourselves. Construction and road
repairs have nothing to do with special guests. They are a

8

matter of routine maintenance with these people!

MUMMUNI
But seriously your Holiness...

CARDINAL
No, no, no. Eminence, my son, Eminence! "Holiness" is reserved for the Pope!

MUMMUNI
Yes, your Eminence! I'm sorry. But you are expected. I'll take you to the authorities.

IMAM
No! You will do no such thing! Not the authorities...

OKOMFO
You see, young man, we don't want to meet the authorities, not yet. We just want a place to spend the night ...

CARDINAL
A simple, humble place, my son ...

MUMMUNI
Oh no! I must take you to the authorities, Holy One ...

CARDINAL
Eminence! My son ...

MUMMUNI
Your Eminence! I am sure they have prepared a fitting place

9

for you at the State House. They don't know that you have arrived ... here ... in Niiman ... of all places. Oh ... No ... Please, come with me ...

OKOMFO
Young man, don't panic. We know what we are doing. We chose to arrive here on purpose.

MUMMUNI
Oh, please ... you will put me into trouble ...

OKOMFO
Do you believe in Him?

MUMMUNI
Who?

OKOMFO
Who indeed! Who else? God! Allah! *Twirediampong Nyakopon!* Do you believe in God?

MUMMUNI
Yes! Yes! Yes! Yes! I believe in God. Of course, I do. I believe in Allah! There is no God but Allah, and Muhammad, peace and blessing upon him, is His messenger!

OKOMFO
Then trust us! We know what we are doing!

IMAM
Yes, Abdul Mumin ... Yes, I know your real full and proper name! We all know it! Who doesn't? Yes, my brother. Find

10

us a simple place ... one room ... here in Niiman. This is where we want to stay.

CARDINAL

We would love to stay in your house, even. Share your room, if that is all right with you ...

MUMMUNI

Wayooyi! Subhana Lahi! ... They want to kill me! Somebody please, help me! The gods want to destroy poor Mummuni!

IMAM

Calm down, my brother, calm down. He means no harm. Surely you can find us a place to stay here in Niiman ...

MUMMUNI
No problem. Just wait here!

(He arranges their luggage which they use as seats. Meanwhile the various ethnic groups have taken positions in separate areas and continue with their music and dancing.)

Please wait for me right here. Don't move. Just sit down and relax. Mummuni will find you a place to stay in Niiman.

(He dashes off and reappears among one of the dancing groups. A mime ensues in which he approaches various individuals to get them to take in the gods. In each case, he is thrown out of the crowd. He finally ends up in "Harlem Cafe." There is cool music playing. HASANA, the prostitute is seated at a table drinking with and talking to a prospective customer.

11

MUMMUNI stands at the entrance and signals her to
come over. She excuses herself from her customer and
walks over to MUMMUNI.)

HASANA
Mummuni! What are you doing here in Harlem Cafe? I
thought you never ...

MUMMUNI
Shh! Come here. Listen to me Hasana! Listen! There is
trouble! Plenty trouble!

HASANA
What is it, Mummuni? What have you done?

MUMMUNI
No, Hasana, it is not me. I haven't done anything. It's the gods!

HASANA
The gods! What gods?

MUMMUNI
Shhh! Not so loud! This is no place to call the names of the
gods in vain! Yes, Hasana. The gods have come! They want
me to find a place for them to stay!

HASANA
Oh, Mummuni, if I did not know you, I would say you have
been drinking. Or have you? Let me smell your breath ...

MUMMUNI
Stop that, Hasana! I am serious. They are here. They want to

stay here! Here in Niiman!

HASANA

So what do you want me to do? Why do you come to me?
What do I know about gods? Please, go away and let me go
and take care of my customer.

MUMMUNI

But Hasana, you know many big, big people. People with
money and property. You know ... like that rich Alhaji who
doesn't know you in the daytime but comes knocking on your
door every night ...

HASANA

Mummuni, please go away. I will lose my customer if I stay
here any longer! Please go on and keep trying. I am sure you
will find a place for them ...

MUMMUNI

Please, Hasana ... Please help me!.... I beg you ...

HASANA

I must go, Mummuni, I will see you later ...

*(The band strikes a new tune and she dances away
seductively, towards her prospective customer.)*

MUMMUNI

Oi, Allah! What do I do now? Can I go to the gods and tell
them I cannot find a single person in this big Niiman to give
them accommodation? What should I do? You ...
(He addresses a member of the audience.)

You there ... you look like a very wise man. Please, advise me. What would you do if you were in my shoes?

(Slowly, the lights fade out. MUMMUNI alone is picked up by a spotlight.)

Eh? Please, I beg you. Somebody, please help me. Do you think I, Mummuni, should invite the mighty gods to spend the night at my place? No please! Don't even think about it. The fact is I don't have a place. I sleep on the veranda of the store in front of Haruna Fulani's house. I swear it is not good. You should see me when it rains. What if it rains tonight? Oh my God. It is already dark! Night is falling and the gods are still sitting where I left them ... waiting for me! I must go back to them. I must tell them something!

(He dashes out. Blackout! Fade-in the gods. The CARDINAL has taken off his shoes. The OKOMFO is pacing up and down. A young GROUND NUT SELLER passes by. They all stare hungrily at her.)

IMAM
Mai Gujiya! ... Mai Gujiya! ...

OKOMFO
Nkatee wura! Hei! Groundnut Seller... Hei Nkatee wura! W'aso asi?... Are you deaf?

CARDINAL
Fine-looking boiled groundnuts! Could we have some, please?

14

GROUNDNUT SELLER
How much do you want?

IMAM
Is it fresh? *(He takes one and tries it.)* Quite tasty but a bit salty. Just a bit salty ...

(OKOMFO attempts to try one but she slaps his hand.)

GROUNDNUT SELLER
Are you buying or you just want to eat for free?

OKOMFO
Hei! Is that how you are? What kind of parents raised you?

CARDINAL
All right, all right, just give us ... er, how much ... ?

IMAM
Ten cedis worth. Let's see how much groundnuts your ten cedis can buy us.

(MUMMUNI enters and rushes to them.)

CARDINAL
Aah! You are back! We were just buying ourselves some groundnuts ...

MUMMUNI
Oh, please help yourselves. How much do they want, Maigujiya?

GROUNDNUT SELLER
Ten cedis worth.

15

MUMMUNI

Oh, give them twenty cedis worth. Here, I'll pay for it.

(He gives her the money.)

CARDINAL

Well, my son, have you found us a place to spend the night?

IMAM

Yes, have you? We are quite tired and would like a good bath and some sleep.

(The GROUNDNUT SELLER leaves.)

OKOMFO

Yes, my feet are killing me. Can we go now?

MUMMUNI

Er ... Most Noble and Illustrious Gods ... I must apologise for keeping you waiting so long, I have been ...

CARDINAL

Don't worry, my son. Just take us to the place so that we can settle down ... I take it you have found us a place, haven't you?

IMAM

Well let's go then!

OKOMFO

I hope it's not too far from here!

(They pick up their luggage and follow MUMMUNI.)

MUMMUNI

Oh, no. It's not far from here. It's Hasana's place. Hasana is a very good friend of mine. Her place is not very far from here. It's just around the corner. It is not the best place ... but ... I am sure Hasana won't mind. She is most hospitable.

CARDINAL

I expect she is expecting us.

MUMMUNI

Not exactly ... but don't worry ... that's all right with Hasana ... she always has guests ... I mean ...

OKOMFO

How much further do we have to walk? My feet are hurting ...

MUMMUNI

Oh, we are almost there. That's Hasana's window. The one with the hurricane lamp hanging in it. That's a good sign ... it means she is at home ...

(Fade in HASANA's room. A sign board reads "HASANA LIVES AND WORKS HERE." HASANA's customer is sitting on a straight back chair and she is sitting astride facing him. They are in semi-darkness. She has pulled up her tight fish-skirt and they are going through the motions of love-making. MUMMUNI and the gods approach the door.)

MUMMUNI

Please, wait here. I must first find out if she is at home... I mean ... decently dressed.

(MUMMUNI knocks on the door.)

HASANA

(Loudly chewing gum and pretending to enjoy making love.)
Are you sure that's the way you want it? Are you sure you
don't want to lie down?...

CUSTOMER

No! No ... No... I like it this way, Hasana. Just shake it,
Hasana. Yaaah! Roll it like you always do for me. Ooooh!
Ahhhh!

OKOMFO

What is that noise? Is the lady all right?

MUMMUNI

(Knocking harder) Hasana! Hasana!

HASANA

Yes!... Yes!...

CUSTOMER

Oooh! ... Hasana ... you are so good ... oooh! ... aah!

MUMMUNI

Hasana ... it's me, Mummuni ... Hasana! Open up!

CUSTOMER

Oh! ... Hasana! ... oooh! ...

HASANA

The door ... somebody is at the door ... somebody is coming
(more knocking) I'm coming ...

MUMMUNI
Hasana! Hasana!

HASANA
I am coming!

CUSTOMER
Oh! God!... Ooh!

MUMMUNI
Hasana! Open the door... it's me...

HASANA
O. K.! I 'm coming!

CUSTOMER
Oh God! I'm coming too! She's coming! Wait ... Ooh, we're coming ... ooh.

(MUMMUNI, thoroughly embarrassed, tries to keep the gods as far from the door as possible. HASANA suddenly realises someone is at the door and springs up. She goes to the door and opens it slightly and sticks her head out ...)

HASANA
Who is it? What do you want? ... Oh, Mummuni what are you doing here?

MUMMUNI
Hasana, I must speak with you. It's urgent! Please send your customer away quickly.

HASANA
Oh, Mummuni ...

MUMMUNI
Shhh ... please not so loud. The gods! They are here with me. Get rid of that fool quickly ...through the window. They must not see him. Do it. Now!

(HASANA closes the door and returns to her customer.)

HASANA
Shh! It's my father. He has a terrible temper and does not approve of my profession or my customers. Please you must leave quickly before he sees you.

(CUSTOMER attempts to leave by the door.)

No! not that way! He'll break your neck! Here, through the window.
(He attempts to climb out through the window.)

Hei!

CUSTOMER
What?

HASANA
My money! You haven't paid!

(The CUSTOMER grudgingly gives her some money and stealthily leaves through the window. She opens the door.)

20

Mummuni! You can come in now.

MUMMUNI
Shh! Is he gone?

HASANA
Yes, of course, he's gone. What is all this about?

MUMMUNI
The gods, Hasana. You have to put them up.

HASANA
Here? In this sinful room? You must be crazy! Please ...

MUMMUNI
Hasana, they are here with me ...

(The gods have already entered the room.)

CARDINAL
Don't worry, my daughter. We are not choosy. We only want a simple abode and this is quite good enough.

(OKOMFO and IMAM are already making themselves comfortable ...)

HASANA
I am sorry, Your Lordship ...

CARDINAL
Eminence! My daughter, Eminence! Not Lordship!

HASANA

Your Eminence, this is hardly a place for people of your high calibre. I am a sinful woman and this room has seen many ...

CARDINAL

Shh! My daughter, leave that to us. It is our problem, not yours!

IMAM

We have not come to judge. That is for our Lord and Master, the Compassionate and the Merciful ...

OKOMFO

So, little girl, forget about sin and get us some water to wash ourselves; some food to eat and we'll be asleep in no time! We will not meddle in your business. I am so tired that when I lay me down, not even an earthquake will disturb my sleep.

HASANA

You heard them, Mummuni! They are our guests for the night. Fetch some water for them. I'll get some food ready!

MUMMUNI
Right away!

(He picks up his water cans and rushes off. The gods get themselves ready for the night. HASANA is busy trying to put together a meal.) Fade-out.

NEXT MORNING
The sun is up. Inside Hasana's room, the gods have finished their breakfast. HASANA is busy clearing away the dishes. MUMMUNI is sitting in a corner quietly finishing his own breakfast.)

CARDINAL
My daughter, you have been very kind to us. So we have decided to take you into our confidence.

IMAM
We are on an inspection tour of certain lands on the order of our Lord and Master. The Merciful One is alarmed by the report reaching Him concerning evil in these lands. Our job is to help determine which land may be saved and which have to ...

OKOMFO
We are so impressed by your behaviour towards us; your hospitality and your generosity have so touched our ... hearts ... that we have decided for your sake ... to give your land a chance.

CARDINAL
We have decided to let "this cup pass you by" ... so to speak. We are supposed to visit many lands. We chose yours first. We are, however, going to ignore what we have seen here and continue on to Lome, Lagos, Nairobi, Harare and notorious Johannesburg before coming back here ...

MUMMUNI
(Throws himself at their feet) Oh, thank you, Great Ones! Allah be praised! We truly appreciate your kindness!

CARDINAL

Calm down, my son. There's no need to be so excited. Hasana's kindness and good nature is highly commendable. But you yourself have also been a very useful instrument; for it was you who led us to the good Hasana.

HASANA

Oh, Your Eminence! You are so kind. You know, I am really not a good girl ... look at what I do to make a living ...

MUMMUNI

And as for me, I am only a good-for-nothing Water-Seller with nothing good to my credit.

IMAM

We know. It is our business to know good from evil ... so, if we say you are good, please don't doubt us ...

OKOMFO

Yes, Mummuni; you are a good man. And you, Hasana you are a very good woman!

CARDINAL

But tell me, my daughter, how are things in this land of yours?...

MUMMUNI

My Lords, we are bad! This whole place is full of evil ...

HASANA

Oh Mummuni, he is not talking to you! Forgive him, your Eminence...

24

CARDINAL

No problem, my daughter. I understand the man. But ... to return to the subject of survival ... how are you managing in this your land? How do the people manage?

HASANA

Er ... we manage, Eminence ... it is not easy but we manage ...

MUMMUNI

It is hard! Things are very hard. You work hard! You try to make honest money ! But you can hardly afford one square meal a day!

CARDINAL

How is that? I thought you are supposed to be rather better off here ... compared to some other places, that is ... I hear the authorities here are doing rather well...

HASANA

Oh yes, Eminence. We are not complaining! I am sure there are some places where things are worse than here. But Mummuni is right. Everybody is complaining. You work and work and work ... I mean work ... I mean not just prostitutes like me, but workers, peasants, labourers, farmers, messengers, even businessmen, doctors, lawyers, engineers, teachers, nurses ... everybody! The pay for one month ... if you are able to stretch it to last two weeks... then you are very lucky indeed!

OKOMFO

Then, supposing you are a lucky one and you are able to stretch your salary to last two weeks ... er ... how do you survive the remaining two weeks? ...

(Both HASANA and MUMMUNI burst into fits of laughter.)

Seriously, I wish to know ... how do you survive?

MUMMUNI
Oh, Respected Gods, that is a very big question, sirs ... it is a question I surely cannot answer ...

HASANA
My Lords ... it's true ... we can't explain ... we manage ... yes we... er ... we manage ...

IMAM
How?

(HASANA and MUMMUNI burst out laughing again.)

HASANA AND MUMMUNI
We manage!

HASANA
It's a mystery. It's like ... like ... everybody knows nobody's money is enough. Yet everybody survives... it's like magic.

CARDINAL
I see!

OKOMFO
Strange!

IMAM
Interesting!

CARDINAL

Anyway, my children, we must go now. As I said, we shall withhold our report until we come back a second time. We hope to see some improvement. Do your best to convince your people to change ... advise the authorities ...

MUMMUNI

Oi! But who are we to advise government people?

HASANA

But Eminence, even the Ministers ... their pay ...

MUMMUNI

How do you know? Are you a minister?

HASANA

Honestly, I think the authorities are trying. You see, your Eminence, I am not trying to be disrespectful; but you, the powerful ones, you have not been of much help yourselves.

MUMMUNI

Hasana!! ... Kneel down, sinner! Kneel down and pray for forgiveness! ... Foolish woman! ... Please forgive her for she knows not ...

CARDINAL

No, no go on! Please speak on, Hasana; I really want to hear you out.

HASANA

You see ... sirs ... I mean, Eminence ... you see ... we all try.

27

The authorities try hardest of all ... but I am sure you remember the bush fires, the long years without a drop of rain that you caused! The deluge of refugees driven out of other lands to come back and try to squeeze crops out of a land that has dried and caked up ... you see ... what I am trying to say is that it is hard now but it was harder before ... thanks to you...!

MUMMUNI

That's true ... and now that the crops are growing and we have plenty of foodstuff ... suddenly the floods are washing away our crops, our houses, even our roads ... Why?... Can't you people manage things a bit better up there?...

HASANA
Mummuniii...Ei! Ei!

(MUMMUNI drops to his knees immediately. The gods begin to laugh.)

MUMMUNI

Forgive me, Holy Ones ... Please forgive me. I did not mean ...

CARDINAL

It's all right, my son ... very amusing! Anyway, my children, we have to go. My son, please bring out our luggage.

(MUMMUNI goes to bring out their luggage.)

Hasana, we are very grateful for your kindness and hospitality. And we are sure you will be able to help bring some change into this land of yours ...

HASANA

But how, Your Eminence, how? How can a poor sinner like me perform this kind of miracle? Oh God, please spare me; please ...

CARDINAL

Don't worry, my daughter, we shall see ... we shall see ... er... my brothers, please come over ...

(The three gods move away and confer for a while. They reach an agreement.)

My child! Come here! Mummuni, take that suitcase and put it aside. We are going, my children, but we shall be back. That suitcase ... with all its contents is yours ... no no, it does not contain clothing ...

IMAM

You can open it only after we have left.

OKOMFO

Everything it contains belongs to you now and you may do what you please with it.

CARDINAL

But, my children use it well and wisely. Use it above all to bring change in this place so that you can save your land. For we have no wish to see the destruction of your land ... no, no ... don't thank us. Farewell. We shall return.

OKOMFO
We shall be back, Hasana.

IMAM
Salaam Alaikum.

(The gods begin to walk off ...)

HASANA AND MUMMUNI
Farewell!

OKOMFO
Ei, Niiman! Interesting ... very interesting ... Niiman ...

IMAM
City-within-a-city. I wonder how they survive! ...

CARDINAL
That was more than a city-within-a-city. It is a land of a million magicians! I wonder what Lagos has in store for us!

(HASANA and MUMMUNI have been watching and waving at the gods. As soon as the gods are out of sight, HASANA and MUMMUNI both dash towards the suitcase. They carry it down.)

HASANA
Are you thinking what I am thinking? What do you think is inside it?

MUMMUNI
Should we open it now? They said we can only open it after they are gone!

HASANA
But they are gone! We can open it now!

MUMMUNI
Yes, let's open it ...

(They open the suitcase and are instantly thrown off their feet by the shock! The suitcase is full of money!)

HASANA
Mummuni!... Mummuni!...

MUMMUNI
Hasana!... Hasana!...

HASANA
Mummuni!... Shhh! ...Calm down ... Mummuni, please do me a favour ... Mummuni!

MUMMUNI
Yes? Ah! I am not deaf ... yes?

HASANA
Mummuni, please do me a small favour. Just take a good look in that suitcase again and tell me what you see inside it.

(MUMMUNI braces himself and takes a close look inside the suitcase. He feels the money, takes out a bundle of notes, rubs it against his cheek and smells it ...)

MUMMUNI
Hasana! ...

HASANA
Mummuni?...

31

MUMMUNI
Hasana, it is money ...

HASANA
Are you sure?...

MUMMUNI
Am I sure?... Here ...

(He grabs her hand and slaps the wad of notes into it ...)

Now, tell me, what is that ... grass?

*(HASANA holds the money, feels it with her hands,
rubs it on her cheeks and smells it ... They fling into
each other's arms ... Music swells up ... and they
dance with joy...)*

HASANA
Mummuni ... Mummuni ... Oh Mummuni, we are rich! We
are also rich!... Mummuni, I want to laugh ... Mummuni, I
want to cry ...Mummuni, I want to sing ... Mummuni, I want
to dance ... Mummuni, I don't know what to do. Mummuni
... we are rich!

MUMMUNI
But Hasana, we must be very careful. This is one big trap and
if we are not careful, we shall fall straight into it.

HASANA
What do you mean, Mummuni? Why would the gods want to
set a trap for two poor creatures like us?...

MUMMUNI

Remember the last thing the big one ... er ... Eminence ... remember what he said?

HASANA

You are right, Mummuni. The gods want us to perform a task for them. They want us to change this place before they come back. Oh, God! Mummuni, can we?...

MUMMUNI

I knew it, Hasana! Those three are too clever for my liking. They are always scheming against poor wretched humans like you and I. Now they have put us into trouble. Plenty trouble!

HASANA

But Mummuni, they have also given us money! Lots of money!

MUMMUNI

Lots of money is lots of trouble, Hasana!

HASANA

But Mummuni, can't you see? Poverty is the root of all our problems in this whole land? With a little money you can solve a few problems.

MUMMUNI

And with lots of money...

HASANA

You can solve many problems!

MUMMUNI

And Hasana, we have more than plenty money in that suitcase. We can solve a lot of problems. But we have no time. We don't know when the gods are coming back.

HASANA

So we must start now. Right now!

MUMMUNI

We must spend the money in the interest of the people! We must spend it in such a way as to bring about the triumph of good over evil in our community!

HASANA

We must use the money to strengthen the poor! We must help the poor of Niiman to resist the terrible temptation to be bad!

MUMMUNI

We must spread our newly acquired wealth around, for it is not ours but the people's!

HASANA

We must feed the people, clothe the people and give shelter to the people so that they can be strong enough to be good ...

MUMMUNI

... And when we have fed, clothed and sheltered them, then we can concentrate on ways to win their souls for the gods ...

HASANA

... Yes ... when we have fed, clothed and sheltered the poor of Niiman, then we ze-e-e-ro in on their spirits and their souls ...

MUMMUNI

...That way ... by the time the gods return, we would have completely transformed Niiman and her people ... We would have transformed this haven of poverty, this citadel of corruption, this empire of sin into a paradise-within-a-city!...

HASANA

...Thus, it shall go down in history and be sung from generation to generation, "How the Gods worked through the sinful Hasana" ...

MUMMUNI
And the wretched Mummuni ...

HASANA

... And saved Niiman, the Land of a Million Magicians, from the wrath of God! From fire and brimstone! And from total destruction!.

MUMMUNI

We must start now, Hasana, for our work is difficult...

HASANA

We must start immediately! Mummuni, we must inform the people about our task and our intentions. We must arrange a big public gathering to launch our campaign! All the people must be there so that they will hear, understand and assist us in our task to save the land from destruction! Then we shall plunge headlong into our work.

MUMMUNI

We shall begin with a party! A big affair! All the people must eat well, sing and dance and be happy. But first we must buy a house.

HASANA

Yes, Mummuni, you are right. We need a decent house. We cannot conduct our campaign from your veranda abode or from my sinful hole.

MUMMUNI

Yes, Hasana. And luckily I know what we can do. The owner of the house on whose veranda I sleep has put the house on sale for sometime now but he has difficulty finding a buyer. We can buy it and convert the store in front of the house into our office and headquarters.

HASANA

Go, Mummuni. Take as much money as you need. Buy the house and convert the store into our office. I am off to arrange the great meeting and festivity.

(Music swells up. MUMMUNI fills his pockets with bundles of money. They lift up the suitcase and as they dance with it, FADE-OUT.

The music splits immediately into simultaneous music of various ethnic groups. When the lights come back, there is a big gathering of the people of Niiman. HASANA and MUMMUNI are seated in comfortable chairs flanked by some of their important guests. Directly above them a sign reads: "HASANA'S BRAND NEW HOUSE AND OFFICE!" One of the ethnic groups is performing a special song composed in honour of HASANA. A woman performs a dance in the middle. She dances up to HASANA who shows her appreciation by pressing many banknotes on the

36

dancer's forehead. There is general applause as
HASANA and MUMMUNI finally join the dance.
Two I.R.S OFFICIALS enter and approach a MAN in
the crowd.)

FIRST I.R.S MAN
My brother, can we speak with you for a minute?

MAN
Who are you? What do you want?

SECOND I.R.S MAN
We are from the Internal Revenue Service. We are here on
Government business.

FIRST I.R.S MAN
Can you tell us where to find Mallam Mummuni and Madam
Hasana?

SECOND I.R.S MAN
We need to speak with them urgently!

MAN
You see that beautifully dressed woman over there? That's
Hasana. And the man standing behind her? That's Mummuni
the water ... I mean the former water seller!

FIRST I.R.S MAN
Can you do us a favour, please. Can you call them out here for
us?

MAN
All right. You wait here.

(The MAN goes and whispers into MUMMUNI's ear. MUMMUNI whispers into HASANA's ear. HASANA gets up.)

HASANA

My people, please excuse us. I have just been informed that some State Officials want to see me. Please, continue to enjoy yourselves. Eat, drink, sing and dance! Mummuni and I will be with you soon.

(MUMMUNI and HASANA leave the crowd.)

HASANA

Gentlemen, I have been told that you want to speak to me. What can I do for you?

MUMMUNI

You are State Officials, I hear. Can I help you?

FIRST I.R.S MAN

(To MAN) Thank you sir, for your kindness. Yes, Mr. Mummuni and Madam Hasana. We are agents of the Internal Revenue Secretariat ...

MUMMUNI

You are the tax people, aren't you? What do you want from the poor people of Niiman?

SECOND I.R.S MAN

Nothing sir, nothing from the poor people of Niiman. It is you we are after.

HASANA
Me?

MUMMUNI
We?

FIRST I.R.S MAN
You are Hasana, aren't you?

HASANA
Yes, I am.

SECOND I.R.S MAN
And you are Mummuni?

MUMMUNI
Na so!

FIRST IRS MAN
Our investigations indicate that the two of you have come into
some money ...

SECOND I.R.S MAN
Quite a fortune we hear...

FIRST I.R.S MAN
We have come specifically to assist you to assess how much
tax you need to pay on your fortune ...

SECOND I.R.S MAN
...And to collect the said tax on behalf of the State ...

FIRST I.R.S MAN

...Thereby assisting you to perform one of your civic duties ...

SECOND I.R.S MAN

...So kindly tell us, what is the size of your total fortune?

MUMMUNI

Err... gentlemen, can you please excuse us for a minute? ... Hasana, come here.

(He takes HASANA aside.)

We must do something. Those people mean business. They are hard and serious.

HASANA

We should tell them how much money we have. Let them assess the tax on it, we pay and that's the end of it ...

MUMMUNI

Are you crazy? Hasana, we can't do that. They will take so much that whatever will be left cannot accomplish our task ...

HASANA

You are right. Give me some money.

> *(He pulls two wads of notes from his big pocket and gives it to her.)*

One more!

> *(He gives her one more wad.)*

Now leave them to me.

(MUMMUNI leaves them and joins the crowd.)

Gentlemen, you wish to know how much money I have?

FIRST I.R.S MAN
And how you made that much money!

HASANA
How much money do you make a month? ... Each of you?...

SECOND I.R.S MAN
Hei! Lady, we ask the questions, not you. You owe the I.R.S.
We collect!

HASANA
Come on, my friends; there is no need to get upset over so
simple a matter ... Just tell me ... truly ... how much do you
make a month? ... As tax collectors ... fifty thousand?

(They burst out laughing.)

One hundred thousand?

(They laugh louder.)

FIRST I.R.S MAN
Sister, listen, don't make fun of us; we are only doing our
job ...

41

SECOND I.R.S MAN

We don't make fifty thousand a month; not even forty ...
but ...

HASANA

But here is five hundred thousand for you and five hundred
thousand for you ... and five hundred thousand for the State.
Now what do you say?

FIRST I.R.S MAN

I say, you are the best and the most law-abiding citizen of this
land! ...

SECOND I.R.S MAN

... And I say you are an angel straight from heaven!...

HASANA

My receipt please ...

*(FIRST I.R.S MAN uses the back of SECOND I.R.S
MAN as "table" to write the receipt.)*

FIRST I.R.S MAN

Your receipt, Madam. You have more than fulfilled your tax
obligations. Goodbye!

HASANA

Won't you join our party? We have plenty to eat and drink.

SECOND I.R.S MAN

Thank you, Madam. You have been kind enough to us.
Another time, maybe. Goodbye.

HASANA
Goodbye and thank you.

(The I.R.S MEN leave. HASANA stares after them for a while and then joins the festivities. Music and dance intensify for a short while and then subside as MASTER OF CEREMONIES takes the floor.)

MASTER OF CEREMONIES
Heeeeey! Heiiiii!!! Brothers and Sisters! People of Niiman ... Guests ...invited and uninvited ... On behalf of Hasana, our sister and Mummuni, our brother, I, Master of Ceremonies, welcome you all to Hasana's brand new house and headquarters. We know that there are many delegations here on behalf of many of our people. Hasana welcomes the distinguished leaders of all the delegations and wishes me to invite them to introduce themselves. First, Magajiya Aisha! Queen of the Prostitutes!

(MAGAJIYA and her entourage of prostitutes take the floor. They do a brief dance which HASANA, unable to control the urge, joins in.)

MAGAJIYA
Hasana, our sister, we thank you for what you have done for us today. We are very happy for you and we wish you long life and more prosperity! For you are one of us! We are proud of you!

(Music swells again and they do another round of brief dancing.)

43

HASANA

(On her knees) Magajiya! My sisters! I thank you. I have called you here not only to rejoice with me but to ask you a favour ...

MAGAJIYA

Ask, Hasana! Whatever you want ... anything ... We shall do ... if we can ...

HASANA

Magajiya, I thank you ... I knew you would be with me. ... I am today launching a campaign to change our land and our circumstances before the gods come back. I want you ... the women of my own profession ... to be in the vanguard of this campaign ...

MAGAJIYA

We are with you! My sisters, are we not with Hasana?

PROSTITUTES

Sure! We are! We'll change Niiman! Long live Hasana!

HASANA

Mummuni will provide all the money you need. We start immediately. Form cooperatives! Build schools ... clinics ... kindergartens ... chop bars ... work! Work for our people and save our land from the wrath of the gods!

(General jubilation. MAGAJIYA and the PROSTI-TUTES dance back to their seats.)

MASTER OF CEREMONIES

Brothers and sisters, on behalf of our sister Hasana, let us

receive and welcome into our midst the leaders of the delegation of beggars... the blind and the seeing, the able and the
disabled ... the sane and the insane ...

*(DELEGATION OF BEGGARS enter accompanied
by special music. They do a brief dance. HASANA
shakes the hands of the leaders.)*

HASANA

It breaks my heart to see what poverty does to our people. It
makes criminals of some of us ... robbing us of our dignity!
My people! From today, ... you must say goodbye to your
begging bowls and calabashes. You will have plenty to eat
and drink ...

*(Suddenly, there is commotion in one corner. A group
has gathered around a young man and are beating him
up.)*

MUMMUNI

Hei ... Hei ... what's the matter? What's going on there?

MASTER OF CEREMONIES

Hei ... Hei ... stop that! Stop that noise and pay attention ...

WOMAN

He's a thief! They are all thieves ... these Tokyo Joe boys! We
caught him re -handed with his hands in my bag. He was trying
to steal my money ...

(Three TOKYO JOE boys are pushed into the middle.)

FIRST TOKYO JOE
She's a liar! Madam don't listen to her!
SECOND TOKYO JOE
Did you see me putting my hands in your bag?

THIRD TOKYO JOE
Don't mind her ... she has nothing in that bag ... nothing ...

(He takes a comb out of his pocket and begins to comb his hair.)
WOMAN
Shut up! You thief! ... You rogue ...

HASANA
My people! This is what I was talking about! This is what poverty has done to us. It's even turned some of us into animals ...

WOMAN
Don't listen to those ruffians, Hasana. Poverty has nothing to do with their behaviour! They are just born like that. They are just ruffians ... they thrive on stealing, hooliganism and wee smoking! ...

FIRST TOKYO JOE
Hei! Be careful woman! You don't know me ... eh?

MUMMUNI
Patience! Young man, have patience.

HASANA
Please, stop this! From now on, we must put ourselves together. We must not allow the gods to come back and find us like this ...

46

(A SECOND WOMAN screams and drags a man by his gown into the middle.)

What is the matter, woman? Why are you dragging the man by his gown? What has he done?

SECOND WOMAN
I caught him! He was stealing food and stuffing it into his pocket ... look inside his pockets ... rice ... meat ... *kose* ... *massa* ... *wagashi* ... fried chicken ... even his mouth is stuffed ... that's why he can't talk ...

HASANA
My sister, let him go ... I say, let the man go! My people, you see what our condition has done to us? When a man is starved for so long, he becomes greedy in the midst of plenty. Deprivation creates thieves. And when a man has been a thief for too long, he steals even from himself! Mummuni!

MUMMUNI
Hasana.

HASANA
Take some more money. Build a big house for all the homeless. They may live in it at no cost ... free ... no rent ...! Buy big buses to convey the men to work, the women to the market and the children to school! This man looks sick ... There are too many sick people in this place. What is the name of that clinic near the round-about?

MUMMUNI
Nyarko Clinic!

HASANA

Yes ... Nyarko Clinic ... Give Dr. Nyarko plenty of money to create more facilities in his clinic to heal our sick. He is not to charge our patients any fees. Tell him to send all bills to Hasana's headquarters for payment. My people, we must organise! We must work hard. We must change Niiman before thegods return! Eat! Drink! Sing and dance! Make yourselves strong and ready! For tomorrow we begin our work!

> *(By this time the crowd is ecstatic with joy! Music and dancing by various groups resume. There is total chaos of sound and movement. FADE-OUT.*

> *SEVERAL WEEKS LATER*
> *Hasana is pacing up and down in her headquarters. MUMMUNI enters, puts his brief-case on a table and slumps into a chair.)*

HASANA

How is it, Mummuni? How are things going? Any improvement in the houses?

MUMMUNI

Hasana, it is getting from bad to worse. The houses are all filthy. Nobody takes care of anything. They don't sweep or clean the rooms. The toilets stink of shit and piss! They chew cola and spit on the walls and on the floors! Nobody listens ... Nobody cares!... Nobody is responsible for anything!

HASANA

It is the same with the transport section! We spent plenty of

48

money to buy many buses. But most of them are already off the roads. Those who ride in the buses have destroyed their insides. Those who drive the buses collude with the fitters and mechanics to steal and sell the parts. ...

MUMMUNI

... And the farms are no better. In spite of good rains, we are just losing everything. Nobody wants to work but everybody talks of more money ... More! ... More!...That's all they want. ... They won't even buy the things we produce ... They spend the money on imported things.

(MAGAJIYA enters.)

HASANA

Aaah! Magajiya, you are welcome.

MAGAJIYA

Hmmm!Thank you, Hasana. How are you?

HASANA

Don't worry about me. How are things on the women's front?

MAGAJIYA

Your sisters are trying but it is hard. Our people are not helping. They are very disrespectful of our efforts. Besides, they steal everything ... books and children's food ... medicines ... anything ... Hasana we have to do something. But why, Hasana? What is wrong with us? What has made us so greedy and self-centered? I don't understand, Hasana! I can understand when a hungry man has to steal in order to feed himself ... but when people feel compelled to steal what belongs to them ... what is their own? ... I cannot understand, Hasana. Can you tell me why?

HASANA
I don't know, my sister. I really don't know. But at least our sisters are trying ... maybe you should give them more encouragement ... more incentives ... who knows ... maybe it is our destiny ... perhaps you and I and our sisters, the prostitutes of this land ... maybe we are doomed to become the saviours of this land ...

MAGAJIYA
Oh Hasana, you must be joking! Anyway, I must be going. I have summoned a meeting of all our sisters and I must not keep them waiting. I will see you later.

HASANA
See you later, Magajiya.

(MAGAJIYA leaves.)

MUMMUNI
Hasana! What are we going to do? We have done everything we can but nothing seems to change. Evil continues to grow. Corruption continues to multiply; our people continue to be bad ... and, Hasana ... what is more ... our money is getting exhausted and ...

HASANA
... And the gods ... the gods, Mummuni!... The gods may be back any moment from now and what do we have to show them?

MUMMUNI

What shall we do, Hasana? ... When the gods gave the money to you ... they gave us and Niiman a last chance ...

HASANA

... And I have failed them. Mummuni, I have failed the gods. ... They put their trust in me and I failed them ...

MUMMUNI

No, Hasana ... please stop crying. You did not fail the gods. The people of Niiman failed you! They and not you have failed the gods ... Please stop crying ... You are breaking my heart ...

HASANA

They will soon return. You heard what they said! They expect change and they depend on us for that change. Nothing has changed ...

MUMMUNI

No. You are wrong, Hasana. Things have changed ...

HASANA

... For worse! Yes! Things have gone from bad to worse. That is no change. That is worse than no change!

MUMMUNI

Hasana ... my dear Hasana, you have changed! Shhh! ... Don't say a word, Hasana. You know, I am right. You were a common prostitute. You used to sell yourself to men of all sorts ... in order to survive ... you don't do that anymore. I was one of your numerous customers. You are so kind that even when I could not pay, you gave me some on credit ... Shhh ... I know ... and I know it was not because you loved me. I was just a customer who sometimes had to buy on credit! ... Now look at you! You have changed completely. You have become a leader of your people ... and you wouldn't let me even touch you ... yes, Hasana, when was the last time you and I did it?... I've been afraid even to ask you ... you have changed, Hasana ... and if I was God, I would not count you amongst sinners ... I would forgive you all your sins ...

HASANA

Oh, Mummuni, you are so kind. You are the only friend I have in this world ...

MUMMUNI

Hasana, I want to be more than your only friend ... I love you, Hasana ... Hasana ... will you be my wife?...

HASANA

...Oh Mummuni, you know I cannot answer that question right now. I am too confused. Besides, this is no time to talk about marriage ...

MUMMUNI

All right, I understand. You need time to think about it ... to find out whether you want to spend the rest of your life with a wretched sinner like me ... whether you can bring yourself to ... to ...

HASANA

Love you? ... Mummuni we have work to do. The gods may be on their way here. We must do something and I have an idea! Will you help me?... Of course! You will! What kind of question is that? Of course, you will help me!

MUMMUNI

What is your idea?

HASANA

It is time to invite my twin brother to help us.

MUMMUNI

What twin brother? You never told me you had a twin brother!

HASANA

That's because I don't have one! I am a twin, yes. That's why I'm called Hasana. But my twin brother died at birth ...

MUMMUNI

Then how can he help us if he died twenty-seven years ago?

HASANA

Because I am going to raise him from the dead ... I plan to use him. Mummuni ... listen carefully, and keep it to yourself. We are going to tell the people that I have a living twin brother who has been away all this time. He has come back but I have to go away ...

MUMMUNI

...Your twin brother is back ... and you have to go...

HASANA

Yes, Mummuni. And while I am gone, he will take care of all my property! You see?

53

MUMMUNI

No, I don't see ... How do you plan to bring him? ...

HASANA

I will not bring him here. I will simply not go anywhere. I will just disguise myself as my twin brother and take care of business on Hasana's behalf ...

MUMMUNI

Yes, I see but how is that supposed to help us? The people will still be what they are ...

HASANA

...That's right ... but I will not be me! I will be my brother. And my brother is mean! My brother is bad-natured and hot-tempered! ... My brother hates dirty people who don't clean houses and who spit on walls! ... He'll kick them out! My brother is a stern businessman ... who wants profit ... He does not care about the gods or kindness or the weakness of the poor. Fuseni will straighten up all this mess!

MUMMUNI

Hasana, it is a brilliant idea!

HASANA

You think so? You really think it will work?

MUMMUNI

I know it will work. Quick, we have no time. Go and disguise yourself. I will spread the word around. Go quickly. Leave the rest to me ... by morning the whole town will know that Hasana has travelled and Fuseni ... her brother who has just

54

returned from far away and long ago is now in charge of Hasana's affairs. Hasana is gone ... and Fuseni is in!

(Black-out as she goes out in one direction and MUMMUNI in another. Slow Fade-in: Hasana's Office. There is a conference table surrounded by chairs. Various people arrive from different directions for an emergency meeting. They include BUS DRIVERS, FARM MANAGER, HOUSING SUPERVISORS, PROPRIETORS, etc.)

FARM MANAGER

I wonder why they've called us all here. They told me it's an urgent and important meeting ...

SUPERVISOR

... They said Hasana has travelled and that her twin brother is here to take care of all the business until she returns ... I never knew Hasana had a brother...

PROPRIETOR

... I never knew either. They say he is very strict and harsh ...

BUS DRIVER

I hope he brought more money! All the buses have broken down ... There are no spare parts and the crowds at the bus stops and lorry parks are growing bigger and bigger!

(MUMMUNI enters followed by FUSENI, 'HASANA in disguise' All stand.)

MUMMUNI

Ladies and Gentlemen, please sit down. It is my greatest pleasure to introduce to you your new boss and director of affairs, Mr. Fuseni. As you may have already heard, Fuseni is our own Hasana's twin brother. He has been gone for a long time but he is now back with ...

MAGAJIYA

The resemblance is truly remarkable ...

PROPRIETOR

... But where has he been all this time?

MUMMUNI

That's not important. The important thing to remember is that Fuseni here is in full control. He directs everything and he decides everything.

FARM MANAGER

Oh Mr. Fuseni, we must express our appreciation for your sister's generosity and kindness to all the people in Niiman ... we hope you will continue the good work she has started ... I am sure my colleagues are with me in ...

(All express agreement through applause, etc.)

FUSENI

My dear friends, I have not only come to continue my sister's good work but to make it even better. I understand that tremendous sums of money have been spread around by my sister ... clearly upon the advice of her dear friend Mummuni.

I am very concerned about how that wealth has been used; for, as you already know, it was made available by the gods, and the gods, my dear friends, expect results when they come back.

MAGAJIYA

... I am sure God will bear witness to how kind and generous Hasana has been ...

FUSENI

My dear sister, I must advise you that the next time you interrupt me, the consequence may not be pleasant for you ... Now ... as I was saying ... I believe my sister has made quite a mess of things! She has a big heart but I am afraid in this world today, a big heart alone does not accomplish much. The gods expect miracles and I am here to give them miracles. Now, we shall start with the buses ... I hear they have all broken down ... is that true?

BUS DRIVER
Yes ...

FUSENI

I can't hear you ... Have the buses all broken down or not?

BUS DRIVER
Yes sir! They have, sir!

FUSENI

Every single one of them? Is that right, Mummuni? ... Surely at least one or two must be running ...

MUMMUNI
It is true, sir.

BUS DRIVER
The last one broke down last week ... and there are no spare parts in our stores ...

FUSENI
Well, go and buy some. Don't you have any money?

BUS DRIVER
No, I don't ...

FUSENI
What?

BUS DRIVER
No! Sir!

FUSENI
What about the money you collect from the passengers... the workers who ride the buses, what do you do with the money?

BUS DRIVER
There is no money, sir. We don't collect money from the passengers, sir. It is free ... they ride on the buses free of charge sir ...

FUSENI
I see! That's great ... that's very generous! Where are the keys to the buses? ... Give them to me! ...

(BUS DRIVER hands over a bunch of keys.)

You are fired! Dismissed. You hear? You and all the other bus drivers, you are all dismissed from this minute ...!

BUS DRIVER
I beg, sir ...

FUSENI
Get out! Get out of my sight! Clear out before I have you arrested!

(BUS DRIVER leaves,)

Mummuni! Here ... take these keys! I want all those buses repaired by the end of this week or by Allah, I'll have you jailed! Sell them to those who care to buy them and who will operate them efficiently and profitably!

MUMMUNI
Yes, sir! But ...

FUSENI
But shut up and do as I say! ... Now you ...

FARM MANAGER
Yes, sir ...

FUSENI
You are the farm manager, aren't you?

FARM MANAGER
Yes, sir! I am, sir!

FUSENI

What are you managing? Grass and weeds? Where are the food crops? ...

FARM MANAGER

Thieves, sir ... the thieves ...

FUSENI

What happened to all the chicken, the eggs, the sheep and the cattle you are supposed to produce to feed the people?

FARM MANAGER

... The people, sir ... they've stolen ...

FUSENI

You are fired! You, your farm hands, your supervisors ... you are all fired! ... Get out of here and evacuate all the farms before sunset ... out! ... Out! All of you, out! Get out of my sight ...

(They panic and begin to scatter.)

You *(to the HOUSING MANAGER)* ... and you, Magajiya ... you stay! I haven't finished with you yet. Are you not in charge of the houses?

HOUSING MANAGER

Yes, sir. I am, sir!

FUSENI

My sister put you in charge of all those big, big houses, did she not?

HOUSING MANAGER

She did, sir.

FUSENI

And she put you and your family in a nice self-contained bungalow so that you can feel comfortable and manage her estates well? Did she not? Answer me ... did she or didn't she?

HOUSING MANAGER

Yes, sir ... er ...sir ... she did, sir ...

FUSENI

How much rent do you pay? ... Do you pay any rent at all? ... Mummuni, all those people ... does any of them pay rent?

MUMMUNI

No sir, Your sister did not insist ...

FUSENI

Mr. Housing Manager, I want the keys to your house by tomorrow morning. You and your family are to pack out immediately ...

HOUSING MANAGER

I am on my knees, sir. Mr. Mummuni, please beg for me. Sir, ... I'll pay rent ...

FUSENI

Get out! Out, I say! ... Get out ...! Mummuni! You are to advertise his post immediately ... with a very attractive salary. I want all the occupants of the houses informed that they are to start paying rent immediately! Those who cannot afford to pay are to be ejected without mercy. From now onwards, you are to place yourself on salary. You are to justify and earn all the money you get!

MUMMUNI
Yes sir! Immediately, sir!

FUSENI
Magajiya!

MAGAJIYA
Yes, sir.

FUSENI
You and all your fellow women ... you especially ... what were you doing for a living?

MAGAJIYA
Lady of the night, sir. I was ...

FUSENI
I can't hear you! What were you before my sister turned you into a respectable women's leader? ... Eh, what were you?

MAGAJIYA
A prostitute, sir. I was a prostitute ...

FUSENI
Queen of the prostitutes ... Magajiya ... that was what you were. A prostitute! You and your band of prostitutes ... you sold your bodies for a living ... is that not true? You fucked men for money!

MAGAJIYA

Your sister herself was one of us, sir. Your own sister was a prostitute too, Fuseni. Hasana also used to fuck men for money ... as you put it ... but we have all changed ... she has been good to us ...

FUSENI

You call this change? No, my sister. You only abandoned one form of prostitution for another. All the money Hasana has spread among the women through you, all those precious resources ... what have you done with them?

MAGAJIYA

We are trying, Fuseni. You judge us too soon ...

FUSENI

It is already too late! You have dissipated the money on frivolous activities. Every woman in this place has become a trader! Nobody wants to produce! To create! To make and to build with their own hands! Everybody wants to buy and sell. "Buy and sell" ... "Buy and sell" ...

MAGAJIYA

I have tried, Fuseni. It is not my fault ...

FUSENI

I will give you one last chance, Magajiya, because somehow, I like you. Tell your women that I have converted all the monies my sister has invested in them into loans! I am prepared to add some more -

MAGAJIYA
Thank you Fuseni.

FUSENI
On condition that they will change their ways. Provided they will cut down on the trading and go into more productive ventures... food production... housing... any kind of production that will bring progress and development to our people. Please go and get to work immediately. We have no time.

MAGAJIYA
Thank you, Hasana ... I mean Fuseni ...

FUSENI
Go, woman! Go, before I change my mind! Out! All of you get out!

(They all leave hurriedly. MUMMUNI staring at FUSENI in total disbelief.)

You too! What are you standing there staring at? Clear out! You goat! Out!

(MUMMUNI runs out. FUSENI paces up and down and then slumps into a chair.)

FADE-OUT.

SEVERAL WEEKS LATER

FADE-IN Hasana's office. FUSENI is pacing up and down. MUMMUNI is counting money with MAGAJIYA's assistance.)

MUMMUNI

You know, Fuseni, you have really achieved wonders these past few weeks. You have put the fear of the Lord in the people.

MAGAJIYA

Mummuni is right, Fuseni. You should congratulate yourself. Everybody is working hard. And we are already making lots of profit.

MUMMUNI

But I am worried. I don't think the gods will approve of our methods ...

FUSENI

But you yourselves told me how worried she was before she left ... because nothing had changed ... Now everything is changing. The houses are all clean, the buses are running. The farms are producing ... and we are even making profit!

MUMMUNI

But there is plenty of grumbling. A lot of people are suffering ... beggars are back on the streets ...

FUSENI

It takes time, Mummuni ... All we need is time ... don't you agree with me Magajiya ...?

MAGAJIYA

I agree. All we need is to keep making more money. We plough the profit back into the projects and it will yield more profits. Slowly but surely we'll take care of everybody ... but I must go. I'm late for the meeting ... I'll see you later ...

(She leaves.)

FUSENI

Thank you, Magajiya ... See you later. Well ... Mummuni, what do you think? How are we doing?

MUMMUNI

I don't know, I am worried. I wonder what the gods are thinking ... they were sent here to investigate ... to help the Almighty to decide whether we should be destroyed or saved. They gave us a chance to save ourselves. They even gave us plenty of money ... we did not succeed one way ... we tried another method ... your method ... I mean Fuseni's method. It seems to work ... I mean, the people are working ... health, sanitation, schools, farms, factories ... many things have improved ... but still there seems to be more poverty ... I mean the poor seem to get poorer and the rich richer ... I don't know what the gods will say ...

(A spotlight illuminates the gods. The impression is that they have appeared out of nowhere.)

CARDINAL

We are not sure ourselves!

MUMMUNI

Oh! My God! Hasana ... I mean Fuseni! ... Oh, they are here...!

IMAM

We thought you were expecting us ... We told you we would be back ...

66

OKOMFO
And we are back!

FUSENI
What Mummuni is trying to say is that we don't think we are ready for you. We don't think we have accomplished the task ...

CARDINAL
We have been debating among ourselves because we, ourselves, are not sure! Many prayers have reached us. Much grumbling from your people. Many have cursed you, Fuseni for making them homeless and jobless and for creating many beggars.

FUSENI
It was the only way ...

CARDINAL
We are not sure, you see, so we have summoned all your people ... we have decided ...

(People begin to gather.)

to set up an open court ... a tribunal of the people ... as it were ... to help us determine your fate and the fate of your land and people.

(More people arrive and begin to help set up a court with the gods as judges.)

Order! Order! Please let us have some order here! This is not one of your open markets. We have not come here to buy and sell. Nor are we here to gossip and peddle rumours ... for which, I hear, this land of yours is famous. We have serious issues to consider ... a soul to judge and the conduct of a whole nation to balance upon the scales of justice. Therefore I pray you, let us have some peace and quiet.

OKOMFO

We passed through this land of yours not too long ago; on a mission on behalf of Him who created the heavens and the earth. We found one good person among all you people ... a woman ... for whose sake we postponed the task of determining whether your land should suffer destruction or experience the mercy of the Almighty. We left good Hasana a modest amount of "means" to accomplish a small task on our behalf ... to multiply goodness and eliminate poverty, suffering and evil. We have returned as we promised we would ... and we ask you to help us judge Hasana and your good selves ...!

CARDINAL

Many are the songs of praise; many still the cries of agony; and yet many times more the curses and wishes of evil upon Hasana and Fuseni. We have therefore called you here to cast your lot on the balance of justice in favour of Hasana for any good work she has done; or against her for any evil she may have committed. For it is Hasana we know. She and she alone shall we hold responsible ... You there ... yes, you ... what do you have to say?

BUS DRIVER

My Lord and Master ... I am a bitter and angry man ... the good Hasana treated me well. I was one of the numerous bus drivers she employed. My colleagues and I ... and our families ... we lived well and happily ... until the good Hasana travelled and her evil brother Fuseni ... that man there, came and took over. From that day we have been jobless, destitute and miserable. He sold the buses to the sharks and business tycoons... we can barely find ourselves one meal a day ... Hasana is good and kind ... it is Fuseni you must punish!

ALHAJI

Punish Fuseni? For what? What has he done? It is true he sacked all of you lazy bus drivers. But he did so because you were pilfering spare parts, running down the vehicles and lining your own pockets. I bought one of the buses, my Lords, and I am proud to say it is on the road everyday, serving our people and getting regular maintenance ...

A WOMAN

Oh sure! And making lots of profit for you! We used to ride to the markets, and our children rode to school free of charge, thanks to Hasana. But you ... every time we blink, you have increased the fares ... Most of us have to walk these days because we cannot afford your fares. I say, hang Fuseni! ... And all the rich Alhajis with him! Hasana is a good woman.

(A crippled MOTHER pushes her way through the crowd. She carries a baby on her back and is followed by three dirty, hungry-looking children in tattered clothes.)

MOTHER

Look at me, respectable ones, look at me and my children. We are penniless and hungry. I am a cripple with four mouths to feed. My husband died in an accident while working on a

69

construction site. The contractor had no insurance. My children and I did not even receive a workman's compensation on my husband's behalf. Our landlord threw us out and we were feeding off the rubbish dumps of Niiman ... until Hasana came. She gave us a place to stay. She fed and clothed us. She gave us back our pride and self respect. Then this ... this ... this monster came. He kicked us out of the house and threw us, helpless, into the streets. Now I sit my crippled self at the street corner at "Thirty-seven." I beg on the street all day. And my little children are reduced to little beggars ... all thanks to Fuseni. Respected ones, Fuseni is a heartless money grabber who does not care about the suffering poor. Punish him, please. Punish him and bring Hasana back!

FARM MANAGER

Fuseni is just a cruel and ruthless profiteer. He does not care who is starving so long as he makes profit ... I don't care that he sacked me. But all the poor farmers and labourers ... simply because we were not making any profits.

FUSENI

Of course, you did not care for yourself! How could you? You had already built yourself a big mansion ... cultivated your own private farm ... and bought yourself a BMW. You were very comfortable... !

HOUSING MANAGER

Must you punish a generation of families for the sin of one man? And all those families you rendered homeless by ejecting them out of their houses ... Hasana was kind and gentle ... She provided food for the hungry and shelter for the homeless ... but you drove them out to starve in the cold streets ...

FUSENI

They had turned the houses into places not fit even for pigs and dogs. They had reduced the entire neighbourhood to a jungle of refuse watered by rivers of piss and shit!

CARDINAL

Magajiya, what about you? What do you say?

MAGAJIYA

Hasana was one of us from the beginning and she remained one of us to the end. She was very good to us ... all of us. She only sought to change the land according to the wishes of the gods ... your wishes ... But my Lords, Hasana was in trouble even before she left. Things were not going very well and she dreaded your return. Fuseni, I am sure, did whatever he did with the best of intentions ...

IMAM

But I hear Hasana evaded tax and indulged in bribery.

SECOND I.R.S MAN

She did it all my Lords, in the interest of the people ... in order to save the money and use if for the people.

CARDINAL

But the State ... does it not also use the taxes in the interest of the people? Besides ... the bribe you took ... in whose interest did you take it?

OKOMFO

Did you distribute it and share it with the people?

FIRST I.R.S MAN

My Lord, forgive us. What we did was wrong but Hasana was good. We insist on that. She did what she had to do because she knew what we and vultures like us wanted. Hasana is good and innocent.

CARDINAL

What about Fuseni? Has nobody anything good to say for Fuseni? Must he be condemned for everything he did? What do you all say?

IMAM

Let us put it to a vote.

OKOMFO

Yes, let's vote.

CARDINAL

All right ... all those who believe Fuseni is a bad man and deserves condemnation, please raise your hands.

(Most raise their hands.)

A clear majority! And all who believe Hasana to be a good and innocent woman ... please raise your hands.

(All raise their hands.)

Yet another majority! It is decided then. Hasana is a good woman and Fuseni is a bad man. Thank you all. We have one more task. We must reward the good and punish the bad. We shall reward the good ... and, according to custom, the bad shall be a carrier for all the evils of your society ... a sacrificial lamb ... as it were. Now, where is Hasana?

IMAM

Will the good Hasana please step forward!

MAGAJIYA

Hasana has travelled, my Lords.

CARDINAL

Travelled? Hasana has travelled? Where?...

FUSENI

No, Hasana has not travelled. Hasana is here with us.

MAGAJIYA

Where is shen then? When did she return?

HASANA/FUSENI
Taking off her disguises and make-up.)

No, Hasana never travelled anywhere. I am Hasana ... and I am Fuseni

ALHAJI
You are Hasana?

FARM MANAGER
... And Fuseni?

ALHAJI
... Hasana and Fuseni ... all in one? Incredible!

MAGAJIYA
You know, somehow I had a strange feeling something was not quite right ... Hasana! Oh, Hasana ... welcome back!

ALHAJI
And you, Mummuni, did you know all the time? ... And you told nobody? ...

HASANA/FUSENI
Please, leave Mummuni out of it. It was all my idea ... Representatives of the Almighty God, people of Niiman ... everybody ... please forgive me. It was all my fault. I took on what was too heavy for me ...

MUMMUNI
No, Hasana, it was not your fault alone ... but ... forgive me gods, you must also share some of the blame. How can you put so heavy a responsibility on ones so weak and frail? ...

74

HASANA/FUSENI

Mummuni, it was my fault. The gods did not force me to accept the responsibility. Besides, whatever Hasana did and whatever Fuseni did ... it was all me! I did them all ...

MUMMUNI

But you were not alone in this, Hasana ... I was with you ... so was Magajiya and you ... and you ... you too ... all of you ... all of us ... we are all part of the problem.

IMAM

But we trusted you ... we believed in you ... all of you ... You have let us down terribly ... we badly wanted to save your land ...

MUMMUNI

Forgive me sirs, but you must admit that you have a part in all this. It is unfair for you to create us ... to create these hostile conditions ... and to drop us ... like fish into boiling water ... and expect us to swim ... Mighty sirs ... pardon me but it is most unfair ... It is easier "for a camel ... no, a whale!" to pass through the eye of a needle ... than it is for us to be good under these conditions ... Please, Mighty Gods ... please forgive me ...

CARDINAL

No, my son ... on the contrary, you may be right ... I do not know. Well, people of Niiman! You have yourselves acquitted Hasana and condemned Fuseni. But as it turns out, Hasana and Fuseni are one and the same person. What shall we do?

OKOMFO

I think we have finished, my brothers. Our task here is done.

IMAM

He is right. We have accomplished our mission ... What happens to Hasana and Fuseni is in the hands of these people ...

CARDINAL

You know, my brothers are right. On our way here, we decided that if we could find one truly good person in this land ... this land shall be saved. And we have found one very good person. There is no doubt about that one, of course. Because everybody here voted and bore testimony to the goodness of Hasana. We must go now.

OKOMFO

We leave you in peace! Do unto Fuseni as you choose ... Your land is saved ... for now ... thanks to Hasana ...

IMAM

... But learn ... people of Niiman ... Learn from the good Hasana ..

MAGAJIYA

Great Ones, we thank you. We will try to be good ... but ... Good sirs ... please permit me to ask a little question.

IMAM

Please, my daughter ... you may ask any question you like ...

MAGAJIYA

With our kind permission, Noble Ones ... I was just wondering ... er ... why Hasana? ... Why give such a heavy burden ... why put it on Hasana? ... And that money ... why did you not give it to the authorities? Is it not the job of the authorities to take care of the people? The poor? ... The hungry? ...The sick? ... The homeless? ... Why poor Hasana?

CARDINAL

My daughter, I am compelled to answer your question with yet another question. Who are the authorities? ... What is authority? ... Where does the power of the authorities come from? ... People of Niiman ... this Niiman and all the other Niimans, the Zongos, the Bukoms, the Harlems and Sowetos all over this wide world ... you are the source of all authority. The power of authority must flow from you. As we leave you, we urge you to wake up and change the nature ... the very essence of authority. For when you have become the source of the power of authority ... only then can you hope to change the conditions in which you live! Hasana, my daughter, we must leave you now. Once more ... farewell and thank you!

(General commotion. HASANA and MUMMUNI rush towards the gods ... but the gods have vanished.)

HASANA

Mummuni, where are they? They are gone, Mummuni. They are gone ...

MUMMUNI

But they were standing right here? My Lord! Illustrious Ones! Where are you? ... They are gone!

(People search in the crowd for the gods but all in vain.)

CROWD

They are gone ... vanished ... They disappeared into thin air ... Wonderful ... it is a miracle ...

HASANA

People of Niiman! You heard them. You heard the gods with your own ears. We must bring change into our land ... but we don't need the gods or their money to do it. We need to organise ourselves to be the source of all the power of authority ... Fuseni ... my ghost brother is gone ... but we don't need him either ... all we need is ourselves ... we must begin now! From now on we shall be the power of authority ...

(The crowd cheers loudly in response to her call to action.)

We shall ensure that all those in authority shall work for our good! Those we put in authority shall be powered and propelled by our needs and our aspirations! From now on let all the authorities take note that we are the source of all authority! ...

MUMMUNI

People of Niiman, please give me your ears for a moment ... Thank you ... thank you all. Hasana, I don't know how to say this. I have been wanting to say it for a long time. But now is the time Hasana, I love you and ... before all these people ... on my knees ... I ask you ... I beg you to marry me!

HASANA

. Mummuni ... oh, Mummuni ... you are a wonderful man ...

MUMMUNI

... Hasana, please be my wife ...

HASANA

I love you too, Mummuni ... but ... but ... no ... not now ... this is
no time to talk of marriage ... We have work to do ... May be
later ... may be after ... my people! People of Niiman, we have
work to do. Don't you agree with me? ...

ALHAJI

What work woman? What is the matter with you? The man
wants to marry you ... he loves you ... don't you see? That has
nothing to do with whatever work you think you have to do ...!

HASANA

But, ... but ... but our work is just about to begin. Can't you
seee? Didn't you hear the gods? We've got to take charge. We
must exercise our power to change the conditions of our lives ...

MAGAJIYA

My sister, you have a chance to settle down with a good man.
You are lucky, Hasana. And I am happy for you.

HASANA

You don't understand. You all don't understand! We have a
chance. A big chance to turn the wheel around and determine
our own direction. I, Hasana! No ... first the gods! Then
Hasana ... then Fuseni ... Do you not see the significance of the
events of the past few months? ... Doesn't all that mean
anything at all to you? Can't you see?

*(The people have already begun to lose interest in
HASANA. They are beginning to carry on their own
conversations.)*

HASANA

My people we are "authority." We are the source of all power. Yet we wade day in and day out in filth and stench. We starve! We have no roof over our heads and barely any clothes on our bodies. And yet the authorities continue to carry on as if we do not exist. We must change the situation, my people, we must!

(The people have started leaving one by one.)

Please don't leave. Don't turn your backs on me. We have work to do. Magajiya, please call them back. Mummuni, I need you ... We have work to do ... please don't go! You can't turn your back on me ... not you, Mummuni.

> *(MUMMUNI turns away from HASANA and takes off his big fancy gown. He walks slowly towards his water containers. He picks them up and, without a glance at HASANA, he walks out.)*

Mummuni! ... Mummuni!... Magajiya, he is gone! Mummuni ... Magajiya ... my sister, they are all gone! What are we going to do? How do we change the land, Magajiya? How? How? How, Magajiya ...!

FADE-OUT

THE END